I0018160

Thank you for purchasing *Windows 7 Fast Start*! We hope you'll look for
other *Fast Start* guides from Smart Brain Training Solutions.

Windows 7
Fast Start

Smart Brain Training Solutions

Copyright © 2014 Smart Brain Training Solutions

All rights reserved.

Table of Contents

1. Introduction

Windows 7 is more customizable than any earlier release of the Microsoft Windows operating system. Powerful features and options combined with traditional favorites allow you to work in new ways. You can perform tasks more efficiently, and you can optimize and customize the operating system in many ways.

Teaching you how to make Windows 7 work the way you want it to is what this book is all about. If you were moving in to a house, apartment, or dorm room, you would want to make the space your own. We do the same with just about everything in our lives, yet surprisingly few people take the time to make their virtual space their own, which can make using a computer a frustrating experience.

One of the ways to make Windows 7 your own is to customize the interface. In any operating system, the interface is everything that connects you to your computer and its basic elements, including the desktop, the menu system, and the taskbar. The way these basic elements look depends on appearance settings. The way they behave depends on customization settings saved in the user profile associated with a particular user account. Because your user account and its associated profile are separate from the profiles associated with

other user accounts on a computer, you can customize the

interface without affecting other users, and your preferred

settings will be remembered and restored each time you log on.

2. Boosting Your Desktop IQ

The desktop is what you see after you start your computer and log on. It's your virtual workspace, and you must master it to begin using your computer faster and smarter.

Optimizing Interface Performance

Windows 7 (with the exception of Starter and Home Basic editions) supports Aero Glass features that provide desktop special effects such as blending and transparency. The Windows 7 desktop with Aero Glass enabled is pretty, but like any cosmetic, its value depends on many factors. The same can be said for the inessential animations and display effects that are enabled by default on most computers running Windows Home Premium or higher.

On older, less powerful computers, you will want to use less of the pretty stuff; using fewer system resources makes Windows more responsive. The same is likely to be true for that new netbook or tablet PC you just bought.

You can optimize the desktop for the way you want to work by following these steps:

1. Click Start, type **SystemPropertiesAdvanced** in the Search box , and then press Enter to open the System Properties dialog box with the Advanced tab selected.

Tip Although there are many shortcuts you can use to access the various tabs and options of the System Properties dialog box, you need not know or remember them all. Instead, pick one technique you like, put it to memory, and use it. The technique I like most is the one mentioned in this step. If the Advanced tab isn't the one I want to work with after I've opened the dialog box, I simply click the tab I want to use, rather than trying to remember that SystemPropertiesComputerName opens the Computer Name tab, SystemPropertiesHardware opens the Hardware tab, SystemPropertiesProtection opens the System Protection tab, and SystemPropertiesRemote opens the Remote tab.

Real World If command memorization isn't your thing but you'd still like a quick and easy way to access System Properties, try this: Click Start, and type **SystemPropertiesAdvanced** in the Search box on the Start menu. Right-click SystemPropertiesAdvanced in the results, and then click Pin To Taskbar. Now the System Properties | Advanced Tab shortcut is available on the taskbar. Whenever you want to access it, simply click the related icon on the taskbar.

---

2. In the Performance section, click Settings to open the Performance Options dialog box, shown in Figure 1. You can now:

- Select Adjust For Best Performance to get rid of all the pretty stuff, or select Adjust For Best Appearance to enable all the pretty stuff.
- Select or clear individual visual effects.

3. Save your changes by clicking OK twice to close both dialog boxes.

The visual effects options that have the biggest affect on performance, in approximate order of impact, include:

Enable Transparent Glass   Controls Window transparency. This might be "flashy," but it is also resource intensive. When off, Windows and dialog box frames are solid.

Animate Windows When Minimizing And Maximizing Determines whether squeezing or stretching animation is used when minimizing or maximizing windows. When off, Windows pop into position.

Fade Or Slide Menus Into View   Controls whether menus fade or slide into view. When off, menus snap open without delay.

Fade Or Slide ToolTips Into View   Controls whether tooltips fade or slide into view. When off, tooltips snap open without delay.

Animate Controls And Elements Inside Windows   Controls the slow-fade effect on buttons and tabs in dialog boxes. When off, buttons glow and tabs open without animation.

Animations In the Taskbar And Start Menu   Controls animations associated with jump lists, thumbnail previews, and sliding taskbar buttons. When off, no animations are used.

Slide Open Combo Boxes   Controls the animations associated with drop-down list boxes. When off, drop-down lists snap open.

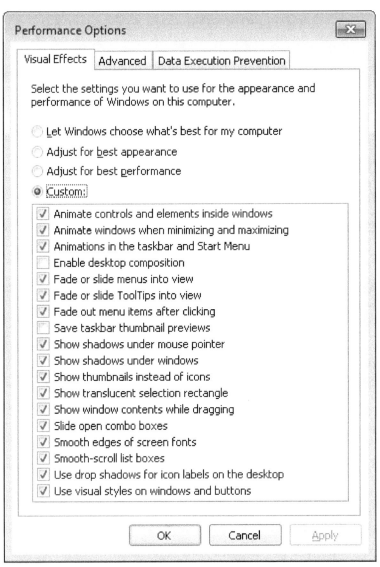

Figure 1 Configuring visual effects to optimize the desktop for the way you want to use it

Real World   The Enable Desktop Composition option ensures that Windows creates a snapshot of each open window in memory before rendering and drawing on the desktop. When you turn this option off, Windows writes directly to the screen, which can improve performance. However, it precludes the use of glass transparency, certain animations, thumbnail previews, and other related features.

Mastering Desktop Essentials

Like a real workspace, the desktop can get cluttered. Programs that you run and folders that you open appear on the desktop in separate windows, and all these open windows can quickly make it difficult to get to the desktop itself. To quickly declutter, you can rearrange open program and folder windows by right-clicking an empty area of the taskbar and then clicking one of the following viewing options:

Cascade Windows   Arranges the open windows so that they overlap, with the title bar remaining visible.

Show Windows Stacked   Resizes the open windows and arranges them on top of each other, in one or more columns.

Show Windows Side by Side   Resizes the open windows and stacks them side by side.

To get to the desktop without decluttering, use the small, blank button on the far right of the taskbar. This button is called the Show Desktop button. You can:

- Temporarily make all open windows transparent by moving the pointer over the Show Desktop button. Restore the windows to their previous state by moving the pointer away.

> **Note** The feature that makes this work is called Aero Peek. Enable Aero Peek and Enable Desktop Composition must be selected on the Visual Effects tab of the Performance Options dialog box.

- Temporarily hide all open windows by clicking the Show Desktop button. Click the button again to unhide the windows and restore them to their previous state.

> **Tip** You don't need Aero Peek or Desktop Composition to show or hide windows in this way. Another way to hide or show open windows is to press the Windows logo key+D.

You can store files, folders, and shortcuts on the desktop for quick and easy access. Any file or folder that you drag from a Windows Explorer window to the desktop stays on the desktop. Rather than placing files or folders on the desktop, you can add a shortcut to a file or folder to the desktop by following these steps:

1. Click Start, click Computer, and then use Windows Explorer to locate the file or folder that you want to add to the desktop.
2. Right-click the file or folder. On the shortcut menu, point to Send To, and then click Desktop (Create Shortcut).

You can also add system icons to the desktop. By default, the only system icon on the desktop is the Recycle Bin. You can add or remove system icons by completing the following steps:

1. Right-click clicking an empty area of the desktop, and then click Personalize.

2. In the left pane of the Personalization window, click Change Desktop Icons. This opens the Desktop Icon Settings dialog box, as shown in Figure 2.

3. Add or remove icons by selecting or clearing their related check boxes and then clicking OK to save your changes.

Some of the desktop icons can be renamed by right-clicking the icon, clicking Rename, typing the desired name, and then pressing Enter. For example, you could rename Recycle Bin as Trash Barrel by right-clicking Recycle Bin, clicking Rename, typing Trash Barrel, and then pressing Enter.

If you no longer want an icon or shortcut on the desktop, right-click it, and then click Delete. When prompted, confirm the action by clicking Yes. Each icon has special options and uses:

Accessing computers and devices on your network
Double-clicking the Network icon opens a window where you can access the computers and devices on your network.

Accessing Control Panel   Double-clicking the Control Panel icon opens the Control Panel, which provides access to system configuration and management tools.

Accessing hard disks and devices   Double-clicking the Computer icon opens a window from which you can access hard disk drives and devices with removable storage.

Accessing the System page in Control Panel   Right-clicking the Computer icon and clicking Properties displays the System page in Control Panel.

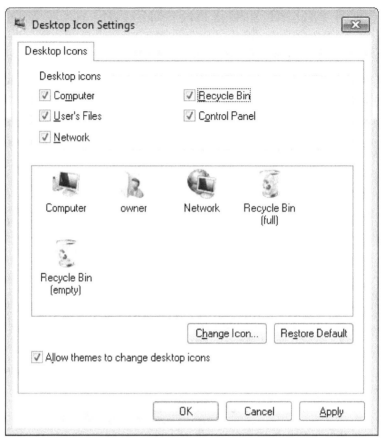

Figure 2 Configuring the desktop icons

Accessing Windows Explorer Double-clicking the folder
icon opens your user profile folder in Windows Explorer.

Connecting to network drives Right-clicking the Computer
icon (or the Network icon) and selecting Map Network Drive
allows you to connect to shared network folders.

Managing your computer Right-clicking the Computer icon
and clicking Manage opens the Computer Management
console.

Removing deleted items   Right-clicking the Recycle Bin icon and clicking Empty Recycle Bin permanently removes all items in the Recycle Bin.

Restoring deleted items   Double-clicking the Recycle Bin icon opens the Recycle Bin, which you can use to view or restore deleted items.

Now that you know how to add items to the desktop, try this:

1. Create a custom Show Desktop button that you can place anywhere on the desktop, open Notepad.exe, type the commands below, and then save the file as Show.scf

```
[Shell]
Command=2
IconFile=Explorer.exe,3
[Taskbar]
Command=ToggleDesktop
```

2. Double-click the related icon to hide or unhide windows.

Stretching the Desktop

Increasingly, desktop PCs and laptops support multiple display devices, allowing you to add a monitor to increase your desktop space. Not only is this a relatively inexpensive way to make your computer more useful, it can also boost your productivity.

Here's an example: You connect two monitors to your computer, or add a monitor as an additional output for your laptop. By placing the screens side by side and enabling multiple displays, you effectively stretch your desktop space and make it possible to view programs and files open on both screens at the same time. Thus, instead of having to toggle between multiple windows, you can have multiple windows open all the time—some on your primary screen and some on your secondary screen.

Typically, if a computer supports multiple displays, it has multiple display adapter connectors. For example, if a desktop PC has three display adapter connectors (two digital and one analog), it likely supports at least two monitors; if a laptop has additional display adapter connectors (digital or analog), it likely supports at least two monitors.

You can confirm the number of supported displays by checking the technical specifications for your display adapter on the manufacturer's website. To determine the type of display adapter on your computer, right-click an empty area of the desktop, and then click Screen Resolution. On the Screen Resolution page, click the Advanced Settings link. The adapter type listed for your display adapter shows the manufacturer name and model information, such as NVIDIA GeForce GT 220.

Getting a computer that supports multiple monitors to stretch the desktop across two monitors is best handled as follows:

1. With the computer shut down (and not in the sleep or hibernate state), connect the monitors to the computer, and then turn on the monitors.
2. Next, start your computer and log on.

Troubleshooting   The logon screen should appear on one of the monitors (although not necessarily on the one directly in front of you). If the logon screen doesn't appear, turn off both monitors in turn, and then turn the monitors back on. If a monitor has multiple modes, such as analog and digital, wait for the monitor to switch to the appropriate mode or manually configure the mode by using the monitor's configuration settings. You may need to wiggle the mouse or press keys on the keyboard to get the monitor to sense the appropriate mode.

3. Right-click an open area on the desktop, and then click Screen Resolution to open the Screen Resolution page in Control Panel, as shown in Figure 3.

Figure 3 Identifying and orienting the displays

4. You have the choice of extending your desktop across the available display devices or duplicating the desktop on each

display (as you might want to do with a laptop). Extend the desktop by clicking Extend These Displays in the Multiple Displays list and then clicking Apply. Duplicate the desktop by selecting Duplicate These Displays in the Multiple Displays list.

5. Click Detect to have Windows display the identity number of each monitor. With two monitors, the displays are numbered 1 and 2. By default, Display 1 always includes the Start menu, taskbar, and notification tray, but you can change this as discussed in the "Making the Taskbar Dance" section.

6. Confirm the display order. Windows doesn't know how you've placed the monitors on your desktop. Instead, it assumes that the primary display device is the first one connected to the display adapter and the secondary display device is the second one connected. It also assumes that the second display is to the right of the first display, which allows you to move the mouse pointer to the right to go from the desktop on the first display to the desktop stretched to the second display.

7. You can tell windows how your monitors are oriented in several ways. If Display 2 is on the left side of Display 1, click the representation of the Display 2 desktop on the Screen Resolution page, drag it to the left past the Display 1 desktop, release the mouse button, and then click Apply. The orientation should now show Display 2 on the left and Display 1 on the right; you can confirm proper configuration by clicking the Identify button. To reverse this procedure, perform the same steps, but drag to right instead of to the left.

8. You can change the monitor that is identified as Display 1 by clicking the representation of its desktop on the Screen Resolution page, clicking Make This My Main Display, and

then clicking Apply. If the monitor you've selected is already Display 1, you won't have this option.

Real World   If you identify and orient the displays incorrectly, moving from the desktop on one monitor to the stretched desktop on the other monitor won't be logical. For example, if Display 2 is physically located to the right of Display 1, but you've incorrectly configured the displays, you may not be able to access the stretched desktop on Display 2 by moving the pointer to the right. Instead, you may need to move the pointer to the left, past the edge of Display 2's desktop, and vice versa.

After you've connected an additional monitor and oriented it properly, working with multiple monitors is fairly straightforward. When you stretch the desktop across two displays, the resolution setting of both displays determines how large the desktop is. If Display 1's resolution is 1920 x 1080 and Display 2's resolution is 1920 x 1080, the effective resolution is 3840 x 1080.

When you maximize windows, they fill their current display from edge to edge. You can click on windows and drag them from the desktop on one display to the stretched desktop on another display. After you click and drag a window, size it as appropriate for the way you want to use it. For many programs, Windows remembers where you've positioned a window when you close it; the next time you open the window, it appears positioned on the appropriate display, as you last worked with it. However, some programs won't remember your preferred monitor, either by design or because the program isn't appropriate for multiple displays.

Any wallpaper you've selected as the background for your desktop will appear on all your displays. Whether you choose a picture position of Fill, Stretch, Fit, or Center, you see a duplicate of the background on each display. When you shuffle background images, the same shuffled image appears on each display as well.

If you want different pictures to appear on each display, you must create pictures at the appropriate resolution, store them in an appropriate folder (such as a subfolder of C:\Windows\Web\Wallpaper), select them as your desktop background, and use the Tile option of the Picture Position list. For example, if Display 1's resolution is 1920 x 1080 and Display 2's resolution is 1920 x 1080, using an art program such as Photoshop, you could combine two 1920 x 1080 images to create one 3840 x 1080 image. You would then store this image in an appropriate folder and select it as your tiled wallpaper.

The standard screensavers that come with Windows 7 also stretch across your displays automatically. There's no need to do anything special to make this happen.

3. Making the Start Menu Work for You

The Start button provides access to your computer's menu system. Clicking the Start button displays the Start menu. You also can display the Start menu by pressing the Windows logo key on your keyboard or by pressing Control+Esc.

As you probably know, and as Figure 4 shows, the Start menu allows you to run programs, open folders, search your computer, get help, and more. What you may not know is how to customize the Start menu so that it works the way you want it to.

> **Tip**   You don't need to click in the Search box before you begin typing. Just type your search text and you'll see any matching results. The Search box also allows you to run programs. Simply type any program name in the box and press Enter to run the program. If you started a search and want to cancel it, click the blue x button to the right of the Search box or press Esc.

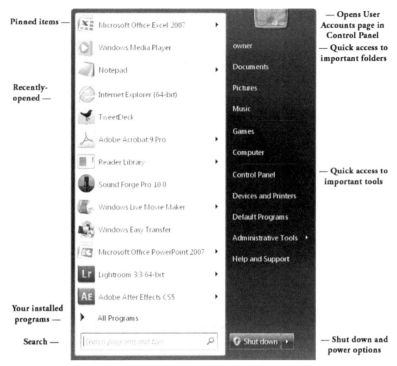

Pinned items —

Recently-opened —

Your installed programs —

Search —

— Opens User Accounts page in Control Panel

— Quick access to important folders

— Quick access to important tools

— Shut down and power options

Figure 4 Getting the most from the Start menu

Customizing the Programs list

The left pane of the Start menu displays pinned programs and recently used programs. You can customize the programs list by pinning items to the Start menu and by changing the number of recently used programs to display.

Programs pinned to the Start menu are listed in the uppermost section of the programs list for quick access to your favorite programs. You can pin a program to the Start menu by following these steps:

1. Click Start, click All Programs, and then locate the program's menu entry.

2. Right-click the program's menu entry and click Pin To Start Menu.

> **Real World**   Sometimes the program you want to pin is not readily accessed in the menu system. In this case, locate the application's executable file (.exe) in Windows Explorer. Right-click the file, and then click Pin To Start Menu.

By default, pinned items are listed in the order in which they are added. You can rearrange pinned items by clicking them and dragging up or down until the desired list position is reached. If you no longer want a program to be pinned to the Start menu, you can unpin it by right-clicking its entry on the Start menu and clicking Unpin From Start Menu.

On the Start menu, recently used programs are listed in the lower portion of the programs list. You can remove a program from the recently used list by right-clicking it and then clicking Remove From This List. However, this won't prevent the program from being added to the list in the future.

You can customize the recent programs list by completing the following steps:

1. Right-click the Start button, and then click Properties.

2. In the Taskbar And Start Menu Properties dialog box, click Customize on the Start Menu tab. Set the Number Of Recent Programs To Display option to the desired value.

3. By using small icons instead of large icons, you can display more programs on the list. Scroll down the list of options and clear the Use Large Icons check box.

4. Save your changes by clicking OK twice.

You can remove the recent programs list and make this extra space available for pinned programs by completing the following steps:

1. Right-click the Start button and then click Properties.

2. Clear the Store And Display Recently Opened Programs In The Start Menu check box, and then click OK.

Customizing the Important Folders And Tools List

The right pane of the Start menu provides quick access to important folders and tools, such as Documents, Pictures, Music, and Control Panel. If you upgraded from an earlier version of Windows, you'll notice that some of the familiar folders don't exist in or have been renamed Windows 7.

In Windows 7, your documents are stored by default in personal folders under %HomeDrive%\%HomePath%. You can quickly open your personal folder by clicking the entry on the Start menu that shows your user name.

Opening your personal folder gives you direct access to its subfolders, such as Documents, Pictures, and Music, so you don't need related entries on the Start menu. Therefore, one way to clean up Start menu clutter is to remove these unnecessary options. If you don't play the built-in Windows games, you can remove the Games options as well.

You can remove features from the Start menu's right pane by using the Customize Start Menu dialog box. Right-click the Start button, and then click Properties. In the Taskbar And Start Menu Properties dialog box, click Customize on the Start Menu tab. In the Customize Start Menu dialog box, you can remove unwanted items in two ways:

- Clear the related check box, such as the Default Programs option.
- Set their related list option to Don't Display This Item.

While you are working with the Customize Start Menu dialog box, you may want to optimize other options as well. Here are some suggestions:

Computer   Display this as a menu so that you can more quickly open specific drives and removable media.

Control Panel   If you're not a fan of Category Control Panel, display this as a menu so that you can more quickly access specific Control Panel utilities.

Devices And Printers   Make sure you select this option, because it is the quickest way to get to your devices and printers.

Default Programs   Clear this option, because you'll hardly ever use it (and if you need it, it is in Control Panel).

Help   Select this option, because it may come in handy in a pinch.

Search Programs And Control Panel   Make sure you select this option, because the Search box is the quickest way to find programs and tools.

System Administrative Tools   If you have appropriate permissions, select Display On The All Programs Menu And The Start Menu so you have quicker access to system tools.

Below the common folder and feature buttons in the right pane of the Start menu, you'll find your computer's Shut Down button. When you click the Shut Down options button (the arrow to the right of "Shut down"), the available options include:

Switch user   Switches users so another user can log on

Log off   Logs off the computer and ends your user session

Lock   Locks the computer so that a logon screen is displayed

Restart   Shuts down and then restarts the computer

Sleep   Puts the computer in sleep mode, if possible given the system configuration and state

Your computer's power configuration determines whether and how sleep mode works. When working with sleep mode, it is important to remember that the computer is still drawing power and that you should never install hardware inside the computer when it is in the sleep state.

4. Making the Taskbar Dance

You use the taskbar to manage your programs and open windows. The taskbar displays buttons for pinned and open items that allow you to quickly access items you've opened and start applications.

Putting the Taskbar Where You Want It

By default, the taskbar is always displayed along the bottom of the desktop on your primary monitor. If you want to move the taskbar to another location, first make sure it is not locked, as indicated by a check mark. To unlock the taskbar, right-click it and clear the Lock The Taskbar option.

After you unlock the taskbar, you can position it wherever you want by clicking on it and dragging. You can:

- Drag the taskbar to the left or right to dock it on the left or right side of the primary desktop. Drag up to dock the taskbar to the top of the primary desktop.
- Dock the taskbar to a location on another monitor. Simply drag the taskbar to the desired left, right, top, or bottom location on the stretched desktop.

After you position the taskbar where you want it, you should lock it in position. To do this, right-click an open area of the taskbar, and then select the Lock The Taskbar option. A check mark indicates that it is locked.

Customizing Taskbar Appearance

You can customize other aspects of the taskbar by using the Taskbar And Start Menu Properties dialog box, shown in Figure 5. To access this dialog box, right-click an open area of the taskbar, and then click Properties. Select or clear options as desired and click OK to save your changes.

The available options include:

Lock The Taskbar   Locks the taskbar in place to prevent accidental moving or resizing. You must clear this option to move or resize the taskbar.

Auto-Hide The Taskbar   Hides the taskbar when you aren't using it and displays the taskbar only when you move the cursor over it. If you clear this option, the taskbar is always displayed (although not always on top), which you may prefer, especially if you move the taskbar around a stretched desktop.

Tip   If the taskbar is hidden and you forget where it is docked, you can quickly display the taskbar by pressing the Windows logo key.

Use Small Icons   Reduces the size of taskbar buttons, allowing more buttons to fit on the taskbar. On my desktop PC, I prefer large icons, which makes them easier to click, but on my tablet PC, I prefer small icons so they take up less screen space.

Figure 5 Customizing taskbar appearance

Taskbar Location On Screen   Sets the relative location of
the taskbar on the currently targeted display. As we discussed
previously, you can move the taskbar manually as well when
it is unlocked.

Taskbar Buttons   Specifies whether taskbar buttons are
always combined, combined only when the taskbar is full, or
never combined.

Use Aero Peek To Preview The Desktop   Enables the peek
feature with the Show Desktop button. If you clear this
option, Windows doesn't temporarily hide all open windows
when you move the pointer over the Show Desktop button.

See the next section for more information on combining buttons and using related options.

> **Note**   Typically, you'll want to combine similar items to reduce taskbar clutter. Rather than displaying a button for each program, the taskbar groups similar buttons by default. Grouping buttons saves room on the taskbar and helps reduce the likelihood that you'll need to expand the taskbar to find the buttons for open programs.

Pinning Programs to the Taskbar

You can pin items that you work with frequently to the taskbar. Pinning an item to the taskbar creates a shortcut that allows you to quickly open a program, folder, or related window.

Pinning items is easy. If you know the name of the program you want to pin to the taskbar, click Start and start typing the program name into the Search box. When you see the program in the results list, right-click it, and then click Pin To Taskbar. From this point on, whenever you want to access the program, simply click the related icon on the taskbar.

Another way to find items to pin is to click the Start button, and then click All Programs. When you find the program you want to pin, right-click the program's menu item, and then click Pin To Taskbar.

To remove a pinned program from the taskbar, right-click its icon, and then click Unpin This Program From The Taskbar. This removes the program's button from the taskbar.

You can set the order of buttons for all opened and pinned programs. To do this, click the button on the taskbar and drag it left or right to the desired position.

When buttons are combined on the taskbar, clicking an item with multiple windows displays a thumbnail with a representation of each open window. You can hover over a window to peek at it on the desktop (as long as the appropriate Aero features are enabled) or click a window that you want to work with to open it. For example, if you open three different folders in Windows Explorer, these items are grouped together in one taskbar button. Hovering over the taskbar button displays a thumbnail with an entry for each window, allowing you to select the grouped window to open by clicking it.

Taskbar buttons make it easy to close windows as well. To close a window, whether grouped or not, move the pointer over the related taskbar button. When the thumbnail appears, move the mouse pointer to the right, and then click the close button for the window you want to close.

> **Real World**   The function of grouping and previews
> depends on whether your computer supports Windows
> Aero Glass and whether Windows Aero Glass is enabled.
> When you aren't using Aero Glass, hovering over an open
> program's button on the taskbar displays a menu with
> icons and titles for each open instance of the program.
> You can still switch to the window by clicking in it or
> close the window by moving the mouse pointer to the
> right and clicking the close button.

Using Flip Views and Jump Lists

Flip views and jump lists are some of the most powerful features of Windows 7. Why? They allow you to quickly get to items that you want to work with.

Display the standard flip view by pressing Alt+Tab. As shown in Figure 6, the flip view contains live thumbnails of all open windows, which are continuously updated to reflect their current state. You can work with a flip view in a variety of ways. Here are a few techniques:

- Press Alt+Tab, and then hold Alt to keep the flip view open.
- Press Tab while you hold the Alt key to cycle through the windows.
- Release the Alt key to bring the currently selected window to the front.
- Select a window and bring it to the front by clicking it.

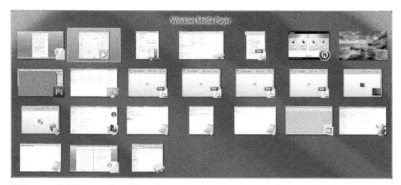

Figure 6 Using the flip view

Display the 3D flip view by pressing the Windows logo key and the Tab key. As shown in Figure 7, the 3D flip view contains a skewed 3D view of all open windows that is continuously updated to reflect the current state. Key techniques for working with 3D flip view are as follows:

- Press the Windows logo key+Tab and hold the Windows logo key to keep the 3D flip view open.
- Press the Tab key while holding the Windows logo key to cycle through the windows.
- Release the Windows logo key to bring the currently selected window to the front.
- Select a window and bring it to the front by clicking it.

Figure 7 Using the 3D flip view

If you think flip views are cool, wait until you try jump lists. Jump lists are displayed after a short delay whenever you right-click and hover with the pointer over an item that has been pinned to the taskbar. When a program's jump list is displayed, you can select a file to open or task to perform simply by clicking it.

Most applications display recently used items or frequently used items. Some applications have enhanced jump lists that also provide quick access to tasks that you can perform with the application. The maximum number of recently or frequently used items on a program's jump list is configurable. By default, jump lists track up to 10 recent items.

You can specify the maximum number of items to display by following these steps:

1. Right-click the Start button, and then click Properties. In the Taskbar And Start Menu Properties dialog box, click Customize on the Start Menu tab.
2. In the Customize Start Menu dialog box, specify the number of recent items to display in jump lists, and then click OK twice.

Windows 7 also allows you to pin items to a program's jump list. To do this, drag an item associated with a program to the program's button pinned on the taskbar and release when the Pin To option appears. Consider the following real-world scenario:

- You want to pin Microsoft Word to the taskbar and pin important documents to its jump list. To pin Word to the taskbar, you click Start, type **Word.exe** in the Search box, right-click Word.exe in the results, and then click Pin To Taskbar.
- After pinning Word to the taskbar, you want to add important documents to its jump list. You open Windows Explorer, locate the first document, drag the document file from the Explorer window to the Word button on the taskbar. When the Pin To Word option appears, you release the mouse button to add the first document to the jump list. You repeat this process to build your list.

Other ways to use jump lists include the following:

- If you pin Windows Explorer to the taskbar, you can add folders to its jump list. To pin Windows Explorer to the taskbar, click Start, type **Explorer.exe** in the Search box, right-click Explorer.exe in the results, and then click Pin To Taskbar. After you've pinned Windows Explorer to the taskbar, simply open Windows Explorer and locate and then drag an important folder from this window to the pinned Windows Explorer on the taskbar. When the Pin To Windows Explorer option appears, release the mouse button to add the folder to the jump list. Repeat this process to build your list.

- If you pin Control Panel to the taskbar, you can add frequently used tasks to its jump list. To pin Control Panel to the taskbar, click Start, type **Control Panel** in the Search box, right-click Control Panel in the results, and then click Pin To Taskbar. After you've pinned Control Panel to the taskbar, simply open Control Panel, locate an important task, and then drag the link for the task to the pinned Control Panel on the taskbar. When the Pin To Control Panel option appears, release the mouse button to add the task to the jump list. Repeat this process to build your list.

5. Customizing Basic Interfaces

You can make Windows 7 yours by personalizing its appearance. From fine-tuning your window colors and experience level to choosing your desktop backgrounds, screen savers, sounds, mouse pointers, themes, and display settings, you can personalize Windows 7 in many ways. Navigating this maze of options can be tricky, however, especially when you want to achieve robust performance while maintaining a desired look and feel.

Many factors can affect your computer's appearance and performance, including hardware components and account controls. You achieve a balance between appearance and performance by making trade-offs when applying personalization settings, yet personalization settings largely determine the quality of your experience.

Of the many interconnected appearance and performance features, you have the most control over the following:

- Basic interfaces and account controls
- Desktop themes, screen savers, and backgrounds
- Personal account settings

In this section and the next, you'll learn how to fine-tune these features while maintaining the balance between appearance and performance.

Windows has many customizable interface features. You can customize your computer's menus, control panels, prompts, and more. This section shows you how.

Personalizing Menus

You'll often use the All Programs menu when you want to work with programs installed on your computer. The All Programs menu lists installed programs followed by a list of folders related to these and other programs on the computer.

Windows 7 manages menus differently than Windows XP and earlier versions of Windows. Windows 7 automatically sorts menus alphabetically as you add, change, or remove menus and menu items; highlights newly installed menus and programs; and opens submenus when you rest the pointer on them. Windows 7 also allows you to view shortcut menus and use drag-and-drop operations on the desktop and within menus.

You control how menus work by using the settings in the Customize Start Menu dialog box, which is accessed and optimized by following these steps:

1. Right-click the Start button, and then click Properties. This opens the Taskbar And Start Menu Properties dialog box.
2. On the Start Menu tab, click Customize to display the Customize Start Menu dialog box, shown in Figure 8.
3. Select Enable Context Menus And Dragging And Dropping to allow shortcut menus to be displayed and to allow dragging and dropping. Clear this option to prevent shortcut menus from being displayed and to prevent dragging and dropping.

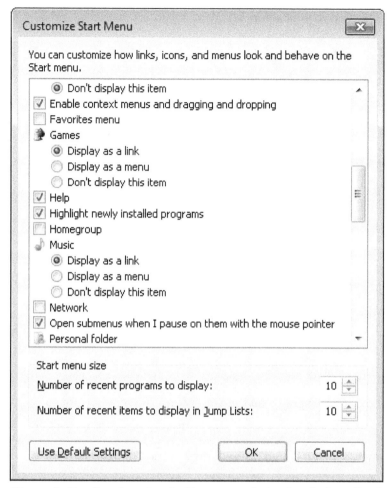

Figure 8 Configuring visual effects to optimize the desktop for the way you want to use it

4. Select Highlight Newly Installed Programs to highlight menus and menu items for newly installed programs. Clear this option to disable newly installed program highlighting.

5. Select Open Submenus When I Pause On Them With The Mouse Pointer to open submenus without clicking. Clear this option to require clicking a submenu to expand it and view its contents.

6. Select Sort All Programs Menu By Name to sort the menu alphabetically by name. Clear this option to show newly installed menus and menu items last.

7. Click OK to save your settings.

Personalizing Control Panel

Control Panel provides quick access to important system utilities and tasks. You can display the Control Panel from any Windows Explorer view by clicking the leftmost arrow button on the Address bar and then clicking Control Panel.

You can toggle views in Control Panel by using the options on the View By list. Category view, accessed by clicking Category in the View By list, shows system utilities by category, utility name, and key tasks. All Control Panel Items view, accessed by clicking Large Icons or Small Icons in the View By list, lists all items in the Control Panel alphabetically by name.

In Category view, all utilities and tasks are accessed with a single click, as with options and programs on the Start Menu. You might want to configure your computer to use the more efficient single-click option to open documents, pictures and other items as well. Configuring single-click open on all items may also help you avoid confusion as to whether you need to click or double-click something.

When you have single-click open configured, pointing to an item selects it and clicking opens it. To configure single-click open, follow these steps:

1. In Control Panel, click Appearance And Personalization.
2. Under Folder Options, click Specify Single- Or Double-Click To Open.

3. In the Folder Options dialog box, on the General tab, select Single-Click To Open An Item (Point To Select), and then click OK.

With everything set to open with one click, you might find that working with Control Panel and Windows Explorer is much more intuitive.

Fine-Tuning Control Prompts

Windows 7 has two general types of user accounts: standard and administrator. Standard users can perform any general computing tasks, such as starting programs, opening documents, and creating folders, as well as any support tasks that do not affect other users or the security of the computer. Administrators, on the other hand, have complete access to the computer and can make changes that affect other users and the security of the computer.

You can easily determine which tasks standard users and administrators can perform. You may have noticed the multicolored shield icon next to certain options in windows, wizards, and dialog boxes. This is the Permissions icon. It indicates that the related option requires administrator permissions to run.

In Windows 7, regardless of whether you are logged on as a standard user or an administrator, you see a User Account Control (UAC) prompt by default when programs try to make changes to your computer and when you try to run certain privileged applications. UAC is a collection of features designed to help protect your computer from malicious programs by improving security.

Generally, when you are logged on as a standard user, you are prompted to provide administrator credentials. On most personal or small office computers, each local computer administrator account is listed by name on the prompt, and you must click an account, type the account's password, and then click OK to proceed. If you log on to a domain, the prompt shows the logon domain and provides user name and password boxes. In this case, you must enter the name of an administrator account, type the account's password, and then click OK to proceed.

When you are logged on with an administrator account, you are prompted for consent to continue. The consent prompt works the same regardless of whether you are connected to a domain, and you must simply click OK to proceed.

The process of getting approval, prior to running an application in administrator mode and performing actions that change system-wide settings, is known as elevation. Elevation enhances security by providing notification when you are about to perform an action that could affect system settings, such as installing an application, and eliminating the ability for malicious programs to invoke administrator privileges without your knowledge and consent.

Windows 7 performs several tasks before elevating the privileges and displaying the UAC prompt, but there is just one that you need to know about: Windows switches to a secure, isolated desktop before displaying the consent prompt, which prevents other processes or applications from providing the required permissions or consent.

Note   Only the prompt itself runs on the secure desktop. All other running programs and processes continue to run on the interactive user desktop.

Elevation, consent prompts, and the secure desktop are the key aspects of UAC that affect you and how you use your computer. To reduce the number of prompts you see, Windows 7 UAC can differentiate between changes to Windows settings and changes to the operating system made by programs and devices. Most of the time, for example, you'll only want to know when programs are trying to install themselves or make changes to the operating system; you won't want to be prompted every time you try to change Windows settings. You also can configure UAC so that the secure desktop is not used.

Real World   UAC can prevent you from installing certain types of programs on your computer. Sometimes you can get around this by right-clicking the program's .exe or other installer file and selecting Run As Administrator. Keep in mind, however, that after the program is installed, it might need to always run with administrator privileges. Instead of right-clicking the program and selecting Run As Administrator every time you want to use it, make the change permanent by right-clicking the program's shortcut or installed .exe file and selecting Properties. On the Compatibility tab, in the Privilege Level section, select Run This Program As An Administrator, and then click OK.

To fine-tune UAC, follow these steps:

1. In Control Panel with Category view, click System and Security, and then under Action Center, click Change User Account Control Settings.

> **Tip** Alternatively, click Start, type **wscui.cpl** and then press Enter. In Action Center, click Change User Account Control Settings.

2. On the User Account Control Settings page, shown in Figure 9, use the slider to choose when to be notified about changes to the computer, and then click OK to save your settings. The available options are:

Always Notify Always notifies you when programs try to install software or make changes to the computer and when you change Windows settings. You should choose this option if your computer requires the highest security possible and you frequently install software and visit unfamiliar websites.

Default—Notify Me Only When Programs Try To Make Changes To My Computer Notifies you only when programs try to make changes to the computer but not when you change Windows settings. You should choose this option if your computer requires high security but you want to reduce the number of notification prompts.

Notify Me Only When Programs Try To Make Changes To My Computer (Do Not Dim My Desktop) Works the same as Default but also prevents UAC from switching to the secure desktop. You should choose this option if you work in a trusted environment with familiar applications and you do not visit unfamiliar websites. You may also want to use this option if it takes a long time for your computer to switch to the secure desktop.

Never Notify Turns off all UAC notification prompts. You should choose this option if security is not a priority and you work in a trusted environment. If you select this option, you must restart your computer for this change to take effect.

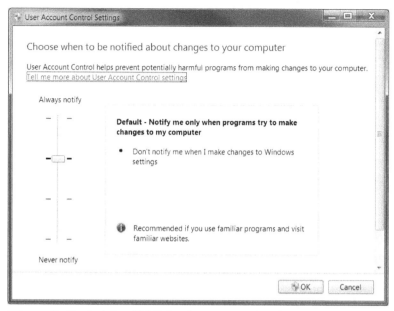

Figure 9 Optimizing UAC for the way you work

Note Depending on the current configuration of UAC, you may
be prompted for permissions or consent. In a domain, you might
not be able to manage UAC by using this technique, although you
may be able to configure individual UAC features in Local
Security Policy, accessible from the Administrative Tools menu:
Under Security Settings, expand Local Policies, and then click
Security Options.

Creating an Alternate Control Panel View

You may have heard about an alternate view for Control Panel that I've

been calling the Ultimate Control Panel. To create an alternate view for

Control Panel, you simply open Windows Explorer and create a new

folder. Give it any name you like, followed by a period and the globally

unique identifier (GUID) for the alternate Control Panel view.

The GUID is: {ED7BA470-8E54-465E-825C-99712043E01C}. For example, you could name your folder:

```
MyStuff.{ED7BA470-8E54-465E-825C-99712043E01C}
```

Or

```
ViewPanel.{ED7BA470-8E54-465E-825C-99712043E01C}
```

Or

```
JustCool.{ED7BA470-8E54-465E-825C-99712043E01C}
```

It's the GUID, not the text string, that does the magic. The GUID is a registered value in the operating system, and it identifies the alternate Control Panel view. When you create and name the folder in this way, you'll have an Ultimate Control Panel that helps you quickly perform common tasks, by allowing easy navigation of many Control Panel options.

Creating a Dedicated Administrator Command Prompt

You use the command prompt to access the Windows 7 command-line interface. If you're a seasoned computer pro, you know this, and you also know that you must elevate the command prompt to perform any administrator tasks. Normally, you do this by accessing Command Prompt from the menu (on the Accessories submenu), right-clicking, and then clicking Run As Administrator. You also can do this by clicking Start, typing cmd.exe, right-clicking cmd in the results list, and clicking Run As Administrator. The result is the same either way: a command prompt that allows you to run tasks that require administrator privileges.

If you pinned Command Prompt to the taskbar, getting an administrator command prompt is a bit more difficult. More difficult, really? Yes, really. To elevate, you must right-click the pinned Command Prompt, right-click Command Prompt again in the jump list, and then click Run As Administrator.

You may be wondering if there is a workaround, and there is. Cmd.exe is stored in the %WinDir%\System32 folder. Locate the file, create a copy by right-clicking Cmd.exe and clicking Copy, and then paste the copy to another folder by accessing the folder, right-clicking, and then clicking Paste. It's a good idea to paste the copy into one of your personal folders, such as Documents.

Next, right-click the copy of Cmd.exe and click Properties. On the Compatibility tab, in the Privilege Level section, select Run This Program As An Administrator, and then click OK. Finally, right-click the copy of Cmd.exe again and click Pin To Start Menu or Pin To Taskbar. Now the pinned copy of Cmd.exe will always run with administrator privileges.

6. Optimizing Desktop Themes, Screen Savers, Backgrounds, and More

You can access personalization settings at any time by using the Personalization page in Control Panel. To access this page, simply right-click on the desktop and click Personalize. As Figure 10 shows, the main personalization settings control the desktop theme used by Windows 7. Desktop themes are combinations of the visual and audio elements that set the appearance of menus, icons, backgrounds, screen savers, system sounds, and mouse pointers. Whenever you switch between themes or modify certain aspects of a theme, you set the user experience level and color scheme for your computer.

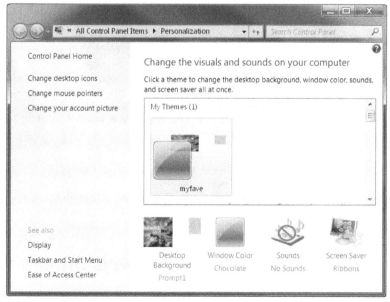

Figure 10 Customizing your computer's themes

In addition to any custom themes you create, several default themes are available. You can apply a default or saved theme by completing these steps:

1. Right-click an open area of the desktop, and then click Personalize.
2. Use the Theme list to select the theme you want to use. If you want to use a saved theme from the Microsoft website, click Get More Themes Online and select the .theme file that contains the saved theme.

Selecting and Tuning Themes

As you've seen, you can switch to any available theme by simply selecting it on the Personalization page in Control Panel. High Contrast, Windows Classic, and Windows Basic are special themes that allow you to forego the pretty stuff to improve performance, which may be necessary on an older computer.

High Contrast themes use only the most basic elements and are designed for people with vision disabilities. Windows Classic and Windows Basic themes reduce the user experience level and appearance substantially. With Windows Classic, you get the look and feel of Windows 2000 while retaining the functionality improvements in Windows 7. This means you'll have a refined Start menu and streamlined Explorer windows, both with integrated search. With Windows Basic, you add gradients and shading, and you get slightly improved performance when working with menus and windows.

When you are using Windows Classic or Windows Basic, you cannot mix colors or configure transparency settings. As a result, clicking Windows

Color And Appearance opens the Appearance Settings dialog box rather than the Windows Color And Appearance page in Control Panel.

You use Windows Standard and Windows Aero themes to enhance the appearance of Windows. Windows Standard is used when Windows Aero is disabled or not otherwise available. Windows Standard supports the Windows Display Driver Model (WDDM) to enable smooth window handling, increase stability, and allow use of Windows Flip. This theme also reduces relics and slow screen refreshes when you are moving user interface elements.

Windows Aero builds on the standard experience by adding Aero Glass, transparency for all windows, live preview, and Windows Flip 3D. However, this theme is only available on a computer running Windows 7 Home Premium edition or higher (and then only when certain conditions are met).

If your computer has an older processor or doesn't have a lot of physical memory, you might want to use the Windows Classic or Windows Basic theme to improve your computer's performance. Although you won't notice much difference between the two, you can use Windows Classic to reduce the overhead associated with drawing gradients and shading.

If your computer has a newer processor and adequate physical memory, you might want to use the Windows 7 Standard or Windows Aero to improve your computer's appearance. The two themes offer very similar user experiences, but Windows Aero delivers more of the pretty stuff.

When you are using Windows 7 Standard or Windows Aero, you can use the Windows Color And Appearance page in Control Panel to change the color of windows, set color intensity, mix colors, and enable or disable transparency.

By default, Windows 7 uses the most advanced theme your computer is capable of using. To change themes, complete the following steps:

1. Right-click an open area of the desktop, and then click Personalize.
2. Select a theme to use by clicking it, and then click Window Color as necessary to fine-tune the colors your computer uses. Note that if you are using the Windows Classic or Windows Basic theme, you will not be able to mix colors or set transparency.

> **Tip**   Want more themes? Visit the themes area in the personalization gallery *http://windows.microsoft.com/en-US/windows/downloads/personalize/themes*.

Fine-Tuning Windows Aero Colors

Windows Aero gives the user interface a highly polished, glassy look. When you use Windows Aero, you can set the glass color, intensity, and transparency by right-clicking an open area of the desktop and clicking Personalize. On the Personalization page in Control Panel, click Window Color.

Several default colors are available, including chocolate (brown), slate (gray), ruby (red), and twilight (blue).While these colors might work for you, you can easily customize the color. Here are some tips to do this:

■ To create softer or bolder colors, select a color and then slide the Color Intensity slider left or right as appropriate.

- By selecting Enable Transparency, you make it possible to see through parts of windows, menus, and dialog boxes. However, this option is resource intensive and may slow down an older computer.
- To get the exact color you want, use the color mixer options: Click Show Color Mixer, and then use the hue, saturation, and brightness sliders to get the exact color you are looking for.

> **Note** The Power Saver power plan automatically disables transparency when running on batteries.

Customizing and Creating Your Own Desktop Backgrounds

If you really want to express your true self, the desktop background can help you do it. The Windows desktop can display a solid background color or a picture as its wallpaper. Windows 7 provides a starter set of background images that you can use as wallpaper.

The default wallpaper images are stored in subfolders of the %WinDir%\Web\Wallpaper folder. For the most part, these images are sized for either widescreen viewing at 1920 x 1200 or standard screen viewing at 1900 x 1440. If you select an image at one of these sizes and your computer monitor has a different display resolution size, Windows resizes the image automatically every time the image is used.

> **Tip** To remove the overhead associated with background resizing, you can size your background images so that they are the same size as your preferred display resolution. If you do this, however, make sure that you save the re-sized images to a new location and then choose this new location. Don't overwrite the existing images.

You can also create background images to use as wallpaper. To do so, simply create appropriately sized images as .bmp, .gif, .jpg, .jpeg, .dib, or .png files, and then add these files to the appropriate subfolders of the %WinDir%\Web\Wallpaper folder. If you do not have access to that folder, or if you would prefer to not make changes to that folder, you can also use pictures from your Pictures Library or specify a folder elsewhere.

> **Note** You should optimize every background image you use. If you don't do this, you risk affecting your computer's performance because Windows will need to resize the image every time it is used.

You can set the background for the desktop by completing the following steps:

1. Right-click an open area of the desktop, and then click Personalize.
2. On the Personalization page in Control Panel, click Desktop Background. This displays the Desktop Background page, as shown in Figure 11.
3. Use the Picture Location menu to specify where to look for the picture you want to use, or click Browse to select a location. Your choices are:

Pictures Library Displays the images in your Pictures library, which is a combination of your My Pictures folder and the Public Pictures folder by default.

Solid Colors Allows you to choose one of the more than 50 pre-defined background colors or create your own background color by clicking More and then using the Color dialog box to select or mix your color.

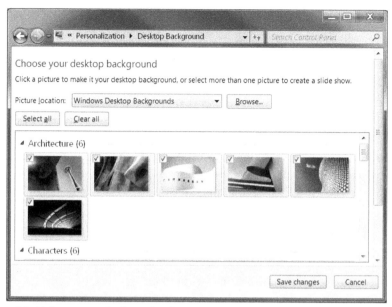

Figure 11 Selecting a desktop background

Top Rated Photos   Displays the top-rated pictures in your Pictures library.

Windows Desktop Backgrounds   Displays the wallpaper images in the %WinDir%\Web\Wallpaper folder.

4. By default, when you select Windows Desktop Backgrounds, Pictures Library, or Top Rated Photos, all related images are selected automatically and the background will rotate among these images every 30 minutes. To deselect an image, clear the check box in its upper-left corner. To select multiple individual pictures, use Shift+Click. You can also select a category heading to select all images in a category.

5. When you are using a background image, you must also use the Picture Position option to select a display option for the background. The positioning options are:

Center   Centers the image on the desktop background. Any area that the image doesn't fill uses the current desktop background color. Click Change Background Color to set the background color for the area the image doesn't fill.

Fill   Fills the desktop background with the image. Generally, the fill is accomplished by zooming in, which may result in the sides of the image being cropped.

Fit   Fits the image to the desktop background. Because current proportions are maintained in most cases, this is a good option for photos and large images that you want to see without stretching or expanding.

Stretch   Stretches the image to fill the desktop background. The proportions are maintained as closely as possible, and then the height is stretched to fill any remaining gaps.

Tile   Repeats the image so that it covers the entire screen. This is a good option for small images and icons (and also to get a single image to fill two screens, as discussed previously).

6. If you are using multiple background images, use the Change Picture Every list to specify how often Windows should change the background image, such as every 5 minutes or every 1 hour. Normally, Windows cycles through the images in order. To cycle through the images randomly, select the Shuffle check box.

7. When you are finished updating the background, click Save Changes.

Real World   When you choose Windows Desktop Backgrounds as the picture location, you see several categories of pictures, such as Architecture, Landscapes, and Nature. These categories are based on the names of the subfolders in the %WinDir%\Web\Wallpaper folder; you can create additional categories by creating new subfolders and adding backgrounds as appropriate to these folders.

Pro Tip   Want to change the background on the logon screen? You can do it, but it's a bit tricky. The logon screen background is configurable by computer manufacturers. If one was created for your computer, it is stored in the %WinDir%\System32\OOBE\Info\Backgrounds folder as background.bmp with default dimensions of 1024 x 768.

Tip   Want more backgrounds? Visit the background page in the personalization gallery http://windows.microsoft.com/en-US/windows/downloads/personalize/wallpaper-desktop-background.

Choosing and Configuring Your Screen Saver

You also can express yourself by using screen savers. Screen savers can be configured to turn on when a computer has been idle for a specified period. Screen savers were originally designed to prevent image burn-in by displaying a continually changing image. With today's monitors, burn-in is not really a problem, but screen savers are still around because they offer a different benefit today: the ability to password-lock your computer automatically when the screen saver turns on.

Windows 7 performs many housekeeping tasks in the background when your computer is idle, such as creating indexes, defragmenting hard disks, creating whole computer backups, and setting system restore points. Although you can install that wild screen saver you've been eyeing, you may want to ensure that generating its images doesn't use resources needed to efficiently perform these background tasks during idle time.

You can configure your screen saver by performing the following steps:

1. Right-click an open area of the desktop, and then click Personalize.
2. Click Screen Saver to open the Screen Saver Settings dialog box.
3. Use the Screen Saver list, shown in Figure 12, to select a screen saver. Although you can install additional screen savers, the standard options are as follows:

   (None)   Turns off the screen saver.

3D Text   Displays the system time or custom text as a 3D message against a black background. (Uses the file %WinDir%\System32\SsText3d.scr)

Blank   Displays a blank screen (a black background with no text or images). (Uses the file %WinDir%\System32\Scrnsave.scr)

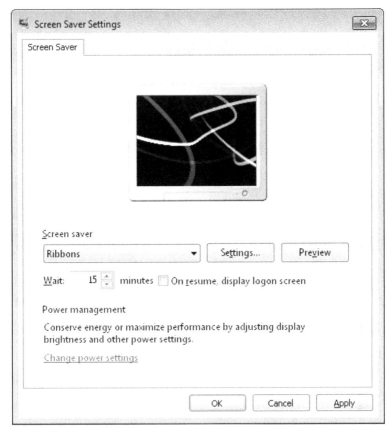

Figure 12 Choosing a screen saver

Bubbles   Displays multicolored bubbles floating across your desktop while the open windows and documents on the desktop remain visible. (Uses the file %WinDir%\System32\Bubbles.scr)

Mystify   Displays arcing bands of lines in various geometric patterns against a black background. (Uses the file %WinDir%\System32\Mystify.scr)

Photos   Displays photos and videos from a selected folder as a slideshow. Make sure you know what images will be shown before you set this up to avoid potential embarrassment. (Uses the file %WinDir%\System32\PhotoScreensaver.scr)

Ribbons   Displays ribbons of various thicknesses and changing lines against a black background. (Uses the file %WinDir%\System32\Ribbons.scr)

4. Password-protect the screen saver by selecting On Resume, Display Logon Screen. Clear this option only if you do not want to use password protection.

5. Use the Wait control to specify how long the computer must be idle before the screen saver is activated. At home, a reasonable value is between 10 and 15 minutes. At the office, you might want to set this to between 5 and 7 minutes. In many offices the Wait setting is set by corporate policy and cannot be changed.

6. Click OK.

The Photos and 3D Text screen savers have additional options (as will just about any custom screen savers you install). The Photos screen saver displays a slideshow of photos, such as your portfolio or family pictures.

To customize the Photos screen saver, follow these steps:

1. In the Screen Saver Settings dialog box, select Photos, and then click Settings to display the Photos Screen Saver dialog box shown in Figure 13.

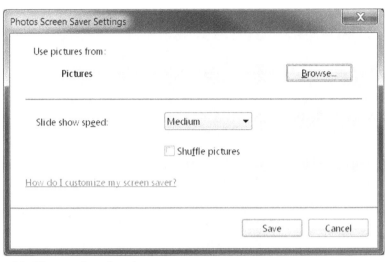

Figure 13 Fine-tuning the photos screen saver

2. By default, this screen saver displays the images in your Pictures library, which is a combination of your My Pictures folder and the Public Pictures folder. To use photos from a different folder, click Browse, and then select the folder you want to use.

3. Use Slide Show Speed list to set the speed of the slideshow. The options are Slow, Medium, and Fast.

4. Photos are displayed in alphanumeric order by default. If you want to shuffle the photos and display them in random order, select the Shuffle Pictures check box.

5. Click Save, and then click OK.

Tip If you've installed Windows Live Essentials and selected Windows Live Photo Gallery, you'll also have the option to use the Windows Live Photo Gallery screen saver. This screen saver functions much like the Photos screen saver, but it includes additional options such as a transitions choices and the ability to specify photos by tag or rating.

To customize the 3D Text screen saver, follow these steps:

1. In the Screen Saver Settings dialog box, select 3D Text, and then click Settings to display the 3D Text Settings dialog box shown in Figure 14.

Figure 14 Fine-tuning the 3D text screen saver

2. Display the current time or a custom message as 3D text. To display the current time as 3D text, select Time. To display a custom message as 3D text, select Custom Text and type your message.

3. Click Choose Font, and then use the Font dialog box to set the font for the 3D text. The default font is Tahoma.

4. Use the Resolution slider to control the display resolution of the text and the Size slider to control the size of the text. The higher the resolution and larger the text, the more processing power required to draw and move the message.

5. Use the Rotation Speed slider to control the speed at which the text moves and rotates on the screen. The faster the rotation, the more processing power required to draw and move the message.

6. Use the Rotation Type list to select the type of rotation to use, such as tumble or spin. Set the rotation type to None to turn off rotation

and reduce the amount of processing power required to draw and move the message.

7. Use the Surface Style options to configure the way the 3D text looks. For example, Solid Color displays the text in a solid color. Click Custom Color and then click Choose Color to display the Color dialog box. Choose the color to use, and click then OK.

8. Click OK twice to save your settings.

Configuring and Creating Your System Sounds

A sound scheme is a set of sounds that you use together. Windows 7 plays sounds in response to a wide variety of events, such as when you log on, when you open or close programs, and when you log off. Programs you install can have their own sounds as well. You manage all of these sounds collectively by using sound schemes.

> Tip   Want your computer to play a snippet from a particular song when you log on or log off? You can do this! When you're configuring sounds for your computer, Windows Logon and Windows Logoff are listed under program events. Simply use any sound editor to create a .wav snippet from the original song files and configure the resulting .wav files for each related event in the Program Events list.

You can configure your system to use an existing sound scheme by completing the following steps:

1. Right-click an open area of the desktop, and then click Personalize.
2. Click Sounds to display the Sound dialog box with the Sounds tab selected, as shown in Figure 15.

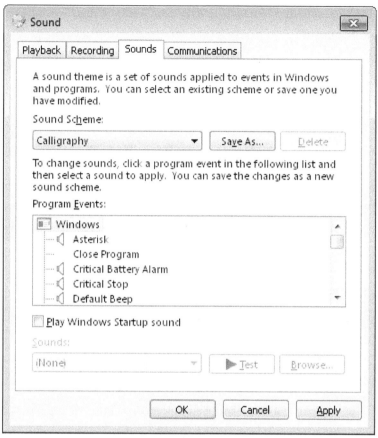

Figure 15 Selecting your system sounds

3. Use the Sound Scheme list to choose the sound scheme to use. Windows 7 has two standard sound schemes:

- No Sounds, which turns off all program sounds except the Windows Startup sound played when you log on.
- Windows Default, which is configured to use the standard Windows sounds.

Note Other sound schemes available typically depend on the edition of Windows 7 installed on your computer and the extras you've installed. Some of the available sound schemes you might see include Afternoon, Calligraphy, Characters, Cityscape, Delta,

> Festival, Garden, Heritage, Landscape, Quirky, Raga, Savanna, and Sonata.

4. In the Program Events list, sounds are organized according to the program to which they relate and the related event that triggers the sound. To preview a sound for a particular event, select the event in the program list and then click Test.

5. To change the sound for an event, select the event in the Program Events list and then use the Sounds list to choose an available sound. You can also click Browse to select other sounds available on the system. The sound files must be in Microsoft .wav format.

6. If you changed the default sounds for a scheme and want to save the changes, click Save As, type a name for the scheme in the field provided, and then click OK.

7. Save your sound settings by clicking OK.

> **Tip**   Want to access the Sound dialog box directly? Click Start, type **Mmsys.cpl,** and then press Enter.

Customizing Your Mouse Pointers

A pointer scheme is a set of mouse pointers that you use together. The three types of mouse pointers you see the most are the Normal Select pointer, the Text Select pointer, and the Link Select pointer. You can configure the appearance of these and other types of mouse pointers and manage them collectively by using pointer schemes.

The available pointer schemes include:

(None)   This doesn't turn mouse pointers off. Instead, it uses nondescript pointers.

Windows Aero   The standard pointers used with Windows Aero settings. Also comes in large and extra-large options.

Windows Black   Inverts the pointer colors so that black backgrounds are used instead of white backgrounds. Also comes in large and extra-large options.

Windows Standard   The standard pointers used with Windows Standard settings. Also comes in large and extra-large options.

You can configure your system to use an existing pointer scheme by completing the following steps:

1. Right-click an open area of the desktop, and then click Personalize.

2. In the left pane, click Change Mouse Pointers to display the Mouse Properties dialog box with the Pointers tab selected, as shown in Figure 16.

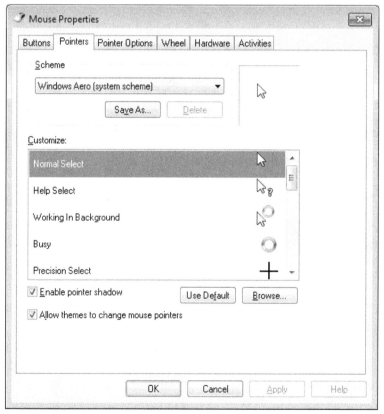

Figure 16 Selecting your mouse pointers

3. Use the Scheme list to choose the pointer scheme to use.

4. In the Customize list, pointers are organized according to their type. To change a pointer, select the pointer and then click Browse. This opens the Browse dialog box with the Cursors folder selected. Choose the cursor pointer to use, and then click Open.

5. If you changed the default pointers for a scheme and want to save the changes, click Save As, type a name for the scheme in the field provided, and then click OK.

6. Save your pointer settings by clicking OK.

> **Tip** To manage mouse settings as well as pointers, Click Start, type **Main.cpl,** and then press Enter. You can now configure mouse buttons, pointers, scrolling, and more.

Saving Your Custom Themes and Creating Theme Packs

So far you have tuned and tweaked window colors, backgrounds, sounds, pointers, and screen savers. Now you'll want to save your settings as a unified theme so you can be sure that you can use it again and again. To do this, follow these steps:

1. Right-click an open area of the desktop, and then click Personalize.

2. On the Personalization page, under the My Themes heading, you'll see Unsaved Theme. Right-click this theme, and then click Save Theme.

3. In the Save Theme As dialog box, enter a name for your custom theme and then click Save. Theme definition files end with the .theme file extension.

4. Unless deleted in the future, the custom theme will appear as a My Themes option. You'll then be able to load the theme simply by clicking it.

A theme you save in this way will only be available to you. That's because the theme is saved in your user profile

(%UserProfile%\AppData\Local\Microsoft\Windows\Themes). If you want to be able to share the theme with others, you must create a theme pack by following these steps:

1. Right-click an open area of the desktop, and then click Personalize.

2. On the Personalization page, under the My Themes heading, you'll see Unsaved Theme. Right-click this theme, and then click Save Theme For Sharing.

3. In the Save Theme Pack As dialog box, enter a name for your custom theme pack and then click Save. Theme pack definition files end with the .themepack file extension and are saved in Libraries\Documents by default. Saved theme packs can be several megabytes in size.

4. Copy the theme pack to a folder accessible to the person you are sharing with. Have the person double-click the theme pack file to load it as a theme and save it to his or her own My Themes list.

Tip   You might be wondering how you delete a custom theme that you no longer want. Well, to do this, select a different theme, right-click the theme you no longer want in the My Themes list, and then click Delete Theme.

Exchange Online

Fast
Start

A Quick Start Guide for Exchange Online,
Office 365 and Windows Azure!

Smart Brain
Training Solutions

XML

Fast
Start

Smart Brain
Training Solutions

www.ingramcontent.com/pod-product-compliance
Lightning Source LLC
LaVergne TN
LVHW052127070326
832902LV00039B/1924